For Doug + Regina,

Ray + Steve.

My other family.

– [illegible]

Rays Friend!

Through the Fire

A Collection of Poems

Dennis L. Markin

VANTAGE PRESS
New York

FIRST EDITION

Published by Vantage Press, Inc.
516 West 34th Street, New York, New York 10001

Manufactured in the United States of America
ISBN: 0-533-10148-4

0 9 8 7 6 5 4 3 2 1

For my family

Contents

I Been Around

I drift all around; I don't know where.
It's been so long now since anyone cared.
I wander everywhere, so far to roam.
Maybe I'm only looking for home.
I'm not just going off for a day
This is a hell of a longer way.
But I know it well and you know it, too;
I will never forget you.

So don't be grievin' when I'm leavin'
And I'm rollin' down the track.
For I will meet you and I will greet you
With a whiskey when I'm back.

I never had a break; what I had I ruined.
I'd better find a niche; I'd better find it soon.
I guess I'm still young, or so I've been told.
But after all those miles, oh, God, do I feel old.
Who can tell me all the answers that I missed
All along that winding road that brought me to this.
This place of pain and sadness, this place of hell.
Oh, love, what is love, come to me and tell.

You're better off with your own kind, surely you
    must see.
Drifter, loner, ne'er-do-well, that's all there is to me.
I wish I was rich and strong; I'd give you everything.
Drop a dollar in my hat, for you I'll sing.
Not too well and out of tune; it's all gone wrong.
Go back to your friends and I'll move along.
Still, it doesn't hurt to dream; it only hurts inside.
Watch for me on a cool grey morning, back to you
    I'll ride.

In Tall Grass

I ran naked in tall grass
After horses, after dark.
Bloody footprints told the tale
Of failure after failure.
The twilight wasn't finished.
It lingered on, as did I.
It's in my head; it's in my body,
In defeat we lie down together.

The northern sickle swung in the sky,
Harvesting souls in tall grass,
Mown down in multitudes.
The guilt was overwhelming.
I, the lowest selfish coward,
Escaped the slaughter that I caused.
I, who longed to ride the horses,
Heard only the thunder of their hooves.

An apple came falling slowly
From a withered branch above.
I rolled to miss it into a pile
Of leavings from my chosen gods.
There I met my nether self,
The bastard king, Prince of Nothing.
Bearing no invasion lightly,
He pushed me back outside myself.

I opened my eyes, there in the grass,
To find myself ringed by my gods.
Silent, unmoving in judgement,
They found me sadly wanting.
Not unworthy; just not ready
To ride to freedom and damnation.
Back inside, I knew humility
As both my friend and purpose.

I ate the wormy apple
So the worm wouldn't die.
He lives inside me, growing fat
On memories of wasted souls.
He stirs impatient on occasion
When thunder rolls like horses' hooves,
As I walk in tall grass
In twilight before a dawn.

A Rich Man

A rich man stopped and gave me a smoke,
Said all I gotta do is tell him a joke.
He'd been around and he'd seen a deal,
But he'd never found a happy time to steal.
I couldn't think of anything funny to tell,
So all I said was, "Welcome to Hell."

He showed ambition and he went real far,
Went to a good school and stayed outta bars,
Climbed the corporate ladder, got a benefit plan.
He married, had kids, and acted like a man.
But his three-piece suit doesn't stay too neat
When he's drunk and busted down on the street.

When any means at all are worth the ends,
You'll do strange things and drive away your friends.
No one will help you; no one will care
When all you've got's a bottle and a head of grey hair.
You got nothing on the drunk lying in a daze
'Cause we all hit bottom in our own ways.

There's a pistol and a bottle in the devil's hands.
For him I'll do anything I can.
No one gives a shit if I live or die.
Every night I hear another lost soul cry.
Rich and poor, we're really all the same.
There are no winners in our evil games.

Long Knives at Midnight

It was amazing, the colour that I saw.
It was terror, stark and complete.
Windows shatter, bodies want for nothing,
Long knives at midnight, big guns at dawn.

Don't lie to me; I can see it in your face.
Don't hold back; your eyes tell the tale.
Wicked little toady of a shabby old madam.
Long knives at midnight, big guns at dawn.

Hideous laughter, cries of glee,
Pain served up in double helpings.
Emptiness is filled; we're lonely all together.
Long knives at midnight; big guns at dawn.

Make my evening with a dirty little look.
Curse and fight me; I like that the best.
Forget all phony morals; accept they don't exist.
Long knives at midnight; big guns at dawn.

Run headlong into pleasure with a drunken stagger.
Left brain or right, it's the wrong path to take.
Muscles pumping fire, leather and lace.
Long knives at midnight; big guns at dawn.

See and hear, smell, touch and taste
Delicious ancient sin, new and improved.
All lovers are junkies, injected and addicted
To long knives at midnight and big guns at dawn.

Sea of Tears

When I hear a voice
In the night you call
I fly away,
There's no world at all.

Just a beautiful girl
With a fire in her eye
Who says to me,
"Don't ever ask why."

Past the clouds and the stars
And the moon so pale,
We're borne aloft
On a heavenly gale.

Comets rush by,
Solar winds blow.
I tell her I love her.
She just says, “I know.”

She lets go of my hand
And I’m lost at sea,
A sea of sadness
And of old misery.

I had this dream
For the first time in years,
A fire girl
And a sea of tears.

Life in Death

I awoke to a dream of life in death
When the waves rolled out their killing thunder,
Crashing at my feet upon the rocks,
Letting me watch an eternal assault.

I crouched beside a bonfire lamp
Flame-tongues licking high, yes, and eager.
To kiss the spray for a taste of salt
And spit out in diamonds, my voyeur's wage.

I trembled at the caress of the wind
That danced over the waves as wild laughter,
Feeding fire its drug in sensual gusts
As it ruffled my hair with tender violence.

I held to the cliff, strong bone of earth
That resisted all advances of wind and wave.
Father of fire and mother of life,
My closest friend the most distant stranger.

I heard the drums of ancient might,
The heartbeat of this world, calling to my own.
On this shore of force and power,
Freedom completed elemental seduction.

I laughed at a dream of mortal worlds
As I arose in the oldest world of all,
To roam forever, the smallest stormcloud
That dreams no more of life or death.

Songs of Love and Passion

Songs of love and passion
Roll through the airwaves all the time.
But they're not the only fashion.
There are other things on our minds.
Order for order's sake,
Mass-produced jobs and homes.
Remember your dreams when you wake
And set them free to roam.

Hey, you, don't be blue.
There're lots of other people asking questions, too.
Hey, you, see it through.
You'll find the answers that really are true.

Try and see yourself from space
Dancing in a storm.
Why bother with the race?
What's weirder than the norm?
Okay, so you're in a maze.
The lie is laid bare.
But you're not just stumbling in a daze,
You're finding your way out of there.

Never mind the mountains of Tibet,
There's happiness to find around here yet.
You could be someone with wisdom to teach,
Lying in the sun on a California beach.

The Anthem of the Night

The last thing that I was thinking to hear
When I came to this city as a kid of too few years
Was the scream and the howl and the screech and
the wail
Of the sirens of cops, ambulance, and fire.
Now that I am older, there's no way I can sleep
Until I hear the lullaby of the anthem of the night.

A spectator's sport, a spectacle of suffering
Is all around me and it's making me numb.
Someone got shot, someone got stabbed
For less money than it takes to buy a decent drink.
A drunk falls down, he's a threat to decent folks.
Better get the boys in blue to chant the anthem of
the night.

I can't help but ask, What's the deal
With the TV people saying they got no time for the
poor?
Living in a false-front, ready-made existence.
Just subtract brains and stir and lap up the sauce.
They drive home from Christmas parties, wrap
themselves around poles,
End a glorious evening with the anthem of the night.

A tenement's on fire with its corpses smokin' sweet.
There's nothing left to save thanks to eighty-year-old
wires.
Four-alarm circus, nothing missing but the popcorn.
Step right up, enjoy the show.
I wish I could stay, but I'm late for the bar.
Let's have another round and sing the anthem of the
night.

Stripped to the Bone

When you saw me staggering and falling down,
Where did you think I was trying to go?

When you heard me slurring my words and
questions,
What did you think I wanted to know?

Oh, how I loved you,
Oh, how I cared.

I could never tell you,
I was always scared.

What a blasted waste, all those years
Laughing 'round a bottle to hide my fears.

I crawled into that bottle, but it fell on its side,
Was under the table with nowhere left to hide.

I did some stupid things, got hauled off to jail,
Cried in my mush, and pissed in my pail.

They gave me fifty dollars, now I'm out at a run.
I'm coming for you, babe, I'm coming with a gun.

Who am I kidding? I'd never hurt you
Just because you don't feel the way I do.

All those old illusions are stripped to the bone.
I point the Magnum this way and I know I'm not
alone.

The Divine Mountain

I climbed the divine mountain
And killed the beast under stars and moon.
I fought the saints and angels
Who never asked nor gave me quarter.
With the blood of ages dripping,
Wings spread over that unhappy height.
The mountain fell beneath me
As I roared out the thunder of the dead.
I rode the wildest wind
To see all kingdoms far and wide.
All who saw my cloud of flame
Knelt and wept for terror and ecstasy.
They did not know me then,
But I was all of them and their desires.
Triumphant yet still lusting,
I drank their dreams and set them free.

Laughing, always laughing
I sold them the deepest, darkest abyss.
Their snarling howls of anguish
Bore me upward in a sky of damnation.
I felt the eye of Heaven
And knew the realm I'd yet to conquer.
Wings spread again, reaching far
To cloak the world in my heart's darkness.
Thus enslaved and forgotten,
Earth I left behind in its melancholy drama.
With flaming sword and heavy spear,
I struck down those lofty gates and towers.
The host, the multitude,
I swept away as leaves in a storm.
I saw the throne of Heaven then
Through the smoke of burning souls.

Destiny had called me
I answered with a rush, a last attack.
Survivors quailed and called me "Lord"
As I ascended those steps of diamond bone.
All but one, alone
Beside the throne he beckoned to me,
To sit in that place,
The highest of all my aspirations.
I saw with his eyes and heard with his ears
All that was and all that would ever be.
My madness overwhelmed me.
I begged for death and cursed eternity.
He held me like a child,
For that I was, his beloved brat.
My fire spent, I fell
Down to Earth and the pit below.

Returned to my flock
Hailed, hailed, I heaped the coals.
Hell's fire thus ignited,
I pronounced judgements in love and kindness.
I inspired all my brethren to the
Uttermost cruelties and punishments unimagined.
I knew nothing of mercy
As the screams echoed across the gulf of worlds.
But I was not happy on that field
Of pain and grief and old regret.
I called forth a power
Ancient and true, the sum of all rage.
Pillars of fire I raised,
Grinning battlements with foundations in suffering.
I built this castle and in it set
Glory, a throne of frozen lightning.

I mounted it and saw with
My own eyes what was and what would be.
I swung open the iron gates
For evil strong and pure, unleashed,
Tricksters some and killers all.
I drove them forward unrelenting low and high.
The wailing of the innocent
Made music with the howling of the damned.
I led the fastest charges
On a steel horse with a heart of death.
With purpose I set sail
Over a sea of blood and broken dreams.
I walked through the foam on a golden shore
And saw, wreathed in mist, the whitest peak.
I climbed the divine mountain
And killed the beast under stars and moon.

Under the Cottonwoods

The killer hatched his plan in the words of a song.
We all loved the music, but we never heard those
words.
He played it under the cottonwoods, near the park
lawn;
People gave him silver as they fed the birds.
Who could have even possibly tried to guess
What he was really thinking as he smiled, sang, and
danced?
He must have thought us tired, in dire need of rest,
For in his terrible melody not a note was left to
chance.

The killer watched his prey—a wolf culling sheep—
Settled on two tender young ones under cottonwoods
at night.
Entranced, they stretched and basked in a lullaby to
sleep;
But the tune pleased not the killer, so he set to make
it right.
Out came the special fork, humming, sharpened
needle-fine.

Notes and bones are all the same, they've got to be
just so.
With much thrashing, writhing, screaming, he then
sat down to dine,
Proud of his new bone harp, so sweet when he plays
it slow.

The killer sang and played, sweetly, ever watchful
For another minstrel's meal and new gut strings by
the way.
Till a curious granny found some parts by the potful
And sped shrieking from the trees, till in prostration
she lay.
The fine new harp was dropped in a sudden anxious
dash,
Then Granny woke in shock, being towed by her hair.
Back towards the cottonwoods for stock in a horrid
mash;
She screamed, but to no end, except her own down
there.

The killer heard the hounds in blue, for sure the end
was near;
No harp now, thanks to Granny, to start a sad
lament.
A broken man, he fondled some bones, and held
them close and dear.
What a way to end, no song in his heart, over the pot
he bent.
Our protectors strong and brave found a sight to
chill the blood.
They wretched and heaved at the parts askew, the
cook as the main course.
Skewered on a strong, young leg bone, à la carte evil

in the mud
As the wind played through the cottonwoods, with a
harper's skill and force.